Reihe Bilingualer Unterricht - Englisch

Young People and the Law

von Dr. Helmut Schütz, Haltern

Abkürzungen:
- **P** Working with pictures or photographs
- **D** Working with data
- **G** Working with graphs or diagrams
- **T** Working with texts
- **A** Working on activities or projects
- doc. document

Ernst Klett Schulbuchverlag

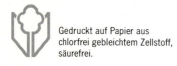
Gedruckt auf Papier aus chlorfrei gebleichtem Zellstoff, säurefrei.

1. Auflage   1 7 6 5 4 3 | 2003 2002 2001 2000 99

Alle Drucke dieser Auflage können im Unterricht nebeneinander benutzt werden, sie sind untereinander unverändert. Die letzte Zahl bezeichnet das Jahr dieses Druckes.
© Ernst Klett Schulbuchverlag GmbH, Stuttgart 1994. Alle Rechte vorbehalten.
Internetadresse: http://www.klett-verlag.de

Redaktion: Dr. Rudolf Erben

Satz: Erhard Perschbacher, Stuttgart
Umschlag: Neil McBeath, Kornwestheim.
Druck: Wilhelm Röck, Weinsberg.
Printed in Germany.
ISBN 3-12-580310-3

Contents

The nature of crime 2
Young offenders 6
A case of shoplifting 12
Legal facts 18
Causes of crime and violence 20
Glossary 28

Introduction

Dear Student,

While this booklet was being put together, two 10-year old boys were found guilty of abducting, torturing and brutally killing a two-year old toddler in Britain. Since then there has been a debate about the treatment of young offenders and the question as to what degree young people may be held responsible for their offences.

This booklet does not attempt to answer this question. Its focus is rather on what may be called 'everyday crime.' The five chapters into which this publication is divided examine the nature of crime, why young people may get involved in deviant and criminal activities, what offences they are found guilty of, and what consequences they will have to face.

Like the other publications in this series for bilingual learners, this booklet is organized around various kinds of documents. These have mostly been taken from the press or official sources, such as crime statistics. Where necessary, complicated legal concepts and questions are explained in more detail. Flow charts and easy-to-follow assignments will guide you through the more complex legal procedures. The English-German and German-English glossary at the end of the booklet lists the technical and more general vocabulary needed for your work.

Although the latest research material has been used, some facts and figures may soon be outdated. You may wish to collect additional material from local, regional and state agencies, as well as press releases to shed further light on a number of issues which have been merely touched upon in this publication.

It has been the author's aim to view juvenile delinquency from two angles, the British and the German. You should feel encouraged to carry out your own research in areas which, for various reasons, had to be neglected here. The local police, courts and social workers in your area will prove helpful with whatever request you may have.

Best wishes

Your bilingual team

The nature of crime

Up against the wall (doc. 1)

Darkhaired dangerous schoolkids
Vicious suspicious sixteen
Jet black blazers at the bus stop
Sullen, unhealthy and mean

Teenage guerillas on the tarmac
Fighting in the middle of the road
Supercharged FSIEs* on the asphalt
The kids are coming in from the cold

High-wire fencing in the playground
High-rise housing all around
High-rise prices on the High Street
High time to pull it all down

White boys kicking in a window
Straight girls watching where they gone
Never trust a copper in a crime car
Just whose side are you on?

Consternation in Mayfair
Rioting in Notting Hill Gate
Fascists marching on the High Street
Cutting back your welfare state

Operator get me the hot line
Father can you hear me at all
Telephone kiosk out of order
Spraycan writing on the wall

Look out listen can you hear it
Panic in the county hall
Look out listen can you hear it
Whitehall up against the wall
Up against the wall

       Tom Robinson Band

---

* FSIE is an abbreviation for a popular car model at the time when the song was written.

T/A Images of young people

1 How does doc. 1 present teenage boys and girls? Look at the first two verses and organise your findings as follows:
a) How are the young people described?
b) Explain what these descriptions suggest about young people's character and behaviour.
c) What impression is created of young people?

2 In what kind of environment do these teenagers grow up? Read the third and the fourth verses and explain how young people might feel about growing up in such cities.
a) How is the environment described?
b) What feeling does the description create?

3 The fifth and the sixth verses try to show how certain groups in society react to what is shown in the first two verses. Find out about this reaction and decide whether it will help to make the situation any better.
a) Describe the reaction mentioned in the song.
b) Comment on that reaction. Do it like this: This will (not) help because ...

The concept of deviance and crime

Many people feel uneasy in the presence of other people who differ from the rest of society. Sometimes this is because of an unusual way of dress; in other cases it is because of differences in the way other people behave. In both cases, these persons become 'suspicious.' If asked, however, most of us would find it difficult to explain why certain forms of dress or behaviour are more acceptable than others. The following definitions may be helpful.

Deviance: a form of behaviour which differs
    from what is generally accepted in society.
    It is often shown by people who want to

Eviction from an empty house (doc. 2)

shock others by simply stepping beyond that invisible border line which divides our society into two groups: those who cling to accepted rules and norms and those who do not.

Deviant behaviour may also be interpreted as some form of protest against conservative ways of thinking or living. Frequently, that kind of behaviour which started as a protest, is finally accepted and is even considered 'normal.'

Some people, however, may strongly disapprove of any kind of deviant and, in particular, indecent behaviour. They would probably consider the action and appearance of the teenagers in doc. 2 offensive and outrageous.

Crime: an act which not only violates a socially accepted norm or code of conduct but also breaks the law. While deviant behaviour is not encouraged in any society, it is not punished as illegal acts are. However, it usually causes little more than a few raised eyebrows or anger. On the other hand, crime and criminal offences are punished.

People are called criminals only if they have broken the law, have been arrested, and have been tried and found guilty by a jury. Crime, in this way, may be considered a form of deviant behaviour which becomes punishable because it is against the law.

Whether certain forms of behaviour are considered deviant or criminal also depends on the circumstances in which they occur.

Just a bunch of hooligans?

4 Doc. 2 shows how young people, who have moved into an empty house, are evicted by the police. Where do these young people fit in the concept of deviance and crime?

(doc. 3)

P C How to distinguish between deviant behaviour and crime

5 Consider the following acts and discuss whether they show milder forms of deviant behaviour or violations of existing laws:

- keeping poisonous spiders as pets,
- sunbathing in the nude in public parks,
- taking a book from the shelves in the public library without having it registered,
- writing graffiti on your neighbour's garden fence,
- smashing street lamps or telephone boxes,
- dyeing your hair crimson and blue to match your green jacket,
- dropping litter in the park,
- forging a signature on a document,
- disposing of chemical waste in the public sewage system,
- pinching a cheap biro from the display in a shop.

6 Look at doc. 3. Describe and comment on the behaviour of the characters shown in the cartoons.

7 Complete the following flow chart. Fill in important characteristics which may help to distinguish deviance from crime.

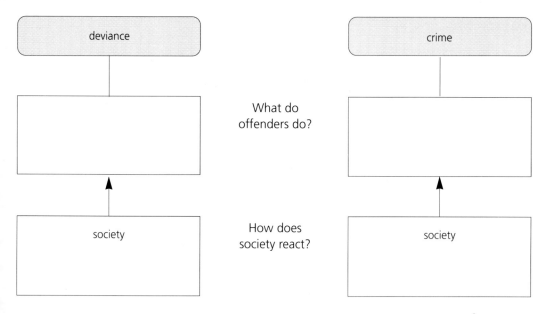

T Summarizing the evidence

8 Fill in the missing words.

a) When people notice different or strange forms of behaviour or appearance, they often feel _____. In some cases, they may even _____ _____ at the way some people behave or dress.

b) Most people cling to _____ _____ or _____ which they expect others to respect as well.

c) So they _____ of a behaviour which differs from that of the majority of people and they call it _____.

d) Especially any kind of _____ behaviour or _____ forms of dress are hardly ever accepted.

e) Crime and criminal behaviour may be seen as a special type of _____, but criminal _____ do not simply _____ certain _____ of conduct.

f) We speak of crime if a _____ has been _____. In contrast to _____ behaviour, which may only cause a few raised eyebrows, criminal _____ are _____ (adj.).

g) People who have _____ a crime are likely to be _____. If they are _____ _____ by a jury, they will be sent to prison or other institutions.

Young offenders

A criminal legend at thirteen (doc. 1)

The following article appeared in The Sunday Times on February 14, 1993. The headline was: 'Darren, 13, rides green lights of the law into criminal legend. Police demand new controls to stop child car thieves.'

A BIG, red felt-tip ring marks Sunday, September 25, 1994, on the forward-planning calendar at Sunderland central police station. It is the day when officers hope they will finally be able to put their most wanted criminal behind bars – the day of his 15th birthday. Until then, they say, the law prevents them from stopping a one-person crime wave called Darren who stands less than 5ft tall from the soles of his trainers to the bristles of his shaven head.

At the age of 13, Darren has a police file an inch thick. He is on the run after absconding from juvenile court more than a week ago and is suspected of driving away more than 200 cars in the Sunderland area in little over six months. When he was kept in care for two days earlier this month, the rate of car crime in Sunderland halved. (...)

"We are waiting and praying for the day this boy reaches 15," said Superintendent Alex Price, chief of police in Sunderland. "The first time he puts a foot wrong, we will be able to deal with him properly."

Darren's record runs to burglary, robbery and assault. But mainly, he steals cars – big, powerful motors which he drives at high speed and uses to ram police vehicles to avoid arrest. His first act on breaking into a car is usually to unscrew the headrest from the driver's seat. He uses it as a booster seat to enable him to see over the steering wheel. He has been arrested more than 40 times since the summer. Each time he has been remanded by the courts into the care of the local social services department because the law says he is too young to be kept in custody. Every time he has got away. (...)

Twice last week police spotted Darren driving big cars. They followed him in powerful vehicles but lost him when he went against the traffic up one-way-streets and drove at speed across wasteland.

A team of plain-clothes detectives went to Darren's tenement estate last weekend to arrest him, but were foiled by 20 of his followers, some as young as seven. The youngsters shouted and whistled warnings as the police moved through the estate. Darren escaped. (...)

Demanding a prompt change in the law, Price said: "There is a hard core of young professional criminals of which this child is the prime example. They are just taking society on. There is no deterrent and they have no fear of retribution. They know when they are arrested they will be home within a few hours.

"Parliament must do something to stop this cancer. I would rather see a 13-year-old car thief incarcerated than see one of my officers pulling him from the wreckage or removing some old lady from under his stolen wheels. This child laughs at our efforts. He has a huge network of contacts and friends who look after him when he is on the run."

T|P Beyond control

1 What makes Darren, a thirteen-year old boy, "the most wanted criminal" in Sunderland? Read doc. 1 and make a list of Darren's crimes.

2 How have the authorities dealt with the boy so far? Why can't the police put an end to this child's criminal career?

3 What, according to the chief police officer, has to be done? Do you think that his suggestions will have the desired effect?

4 Describe doc. 2. What could be the motivation behind the teenager's action?

Just an exception?

Although the thought of thirteen-year olds breaking into cars and stealing them is worrying enough, one might think that these are exceptions. Official criminal statistics tell a different story. To be able to read and understand them properly we must first take a look at a number of definitions.

The German police, who keep records of people who are suspected of having broken the law, divide society into various age groups. Although children below the age of 14 cannot be held responsible for what they do, they figure in police statistics of suspects. Adolescents of 14 to 18 years of age, who will face milder forms of punishment if convicted, are another group. Those beetween 18 and 21, the older adolescents, may be punished even more severely. Finally, adult criminals of 21 and older are regarded fully responsible for what they do. For some reason, young adults of 21 to 25 years of age also appear to be an important group in police statistics.

The pie chart on the following page (doc. 3) shows the percentage of suspects in Germany.

G Who dunnit?

5 Complete doc. 3 on the following page. Enter the various ages into the diagram.

6 Find out the percentage of all age groups below 21 years of age.

Car wreck after a joyride (doc. 2)

Age groups of suspects in Germany, 1991 (doc. 3)

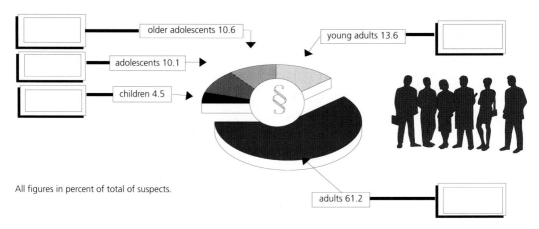

All figures in percent of total of suspects.

G Offenders in England and Wales

7 In doc. 4, which age group has the highest number of offenders? Which age group has the lowest number?

8 What age group shows little change in the number of offenders? What general trend can be noticed?

Male offenders in British criminal statistics, 1979-1989 (doc. 4)

The graph shows the changing numbers of male offenders in England and Wales. The bars represent particular age groups which you can look up in the key. All figures are in thousands.

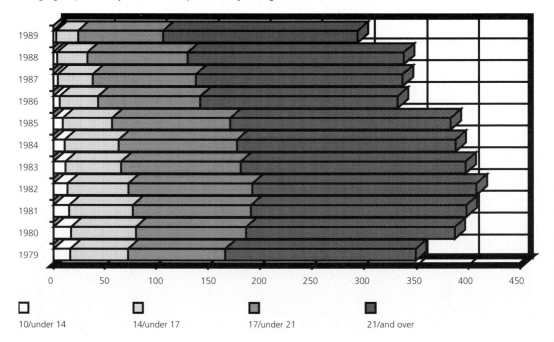

Suspects in German criminal statistics, 1991 (doc. 5)

age groups	suspects (total)	male suspects	female suspects
children	65,205	50,370	14,835
adolescents	139,709	109,768	29,941
older adolescents	150,286	123,824	26,462
adults	1,111,552	852,973	258,579

D A Suspects in criminal statistics

9 Before you start working with doc. 5, re-read the definiton of age groups in the text 'Just an exception?' on page 7.

10 Use the data in doc. 5 to draw a bar graph which shows the proportions of individual groups of suspects (total only).

11 Draw a pie chart which shows proportions of male and female suspects.

12 Do you think that the statistics in docs. 4 and 5 allow for any comparative study of crime in Britain and Germany?
Consider the following definitions of offenders and suspects.

Offenders and suspects

Offender: a person who has committed a crime and been found guilty of having done so by a court. It is only after a person has been convicted of committing an offence in the course of court procedures that he or she may be treated as a criminal.

Suspect: a person who, as a consequence of police investigations, may be suspected of – but not considered guilty of – having committed a crime.
In Germany, counts of suspects include persons who cannot be held responsible under criminal law, for example children under 14.

T Sunderland's terrible child

13 Fill in the missing words.

a) The last time Darren had to appear at a _____ court, he _____ and has been on the run ever since.

b) He is a one-person _____ _____ and when he was _____ __ _____ for two days earlier this month, the _____ of car crime halved.

c) Whenever he was arrested by the police, he was _____ into the care of the local _____ _____ _____ by the courts.

d) He is too young to be _____ __ _____ .

e) The police say that there is a hard _____ of young offenders who commit their crimes because they fear no _____.

f) The police believe these criminals should be _____ in order to make the streets safe again.

(doc. 6)

(doc. 7)

Labelling

People often feel that others have formed some sort of picture of them, a conception of what they are like, what traits of character they have. One is hardly aware of how this conception is formed, yet it is based on the observation of actual behaviour as well as on things one may have said in one situation or other. After some time this conception of your personality is turned into a label: You are no longer what you think you are, but you are the personality that people around you believe you to be.

There may have been situations in which you forgot to do your homework and your teachers found out about it. On many other occasions you may have done it, but you were not asked to present it in class. And then again, one day you fail to produce your homework because your brother or sister took your exercise-book instead of his or hers. As a result, your teacher may see you as lazy and unreliable. It is then that you have been labelled. Labels attached to other pupils can be 'troublemaker,' 'dreamer' or 'bully.'

In most cases these labels have a negative meaning. They usually describe in what way persons are different from others or how much they have failed to follow the rules which have been set by those who label them. These are deviant labels. Although they may be based on observation and experience, they are also stereotypes which do not take into consideration people's full personality and individuality.

Who labels whom?

There are some groups in society that have more power than others to label people or their behaviour as deviant. One of these are the police. Of course, people are no longer locked into the pillory if they have done something wrong so that they can be publicly ridiculed. Doc. 7 shows how it was done three hundred years ago. However, labelling still takes place, as doc. 6 shows.

Police instruction material (doc. 8)

According to one piece of police instruction material, the following persons should be regarded as suspicious:
- young people generally, but especially in cars (or groups of cars);
- people in badly-maintained cars, especially if they have a tatty, dog-eared licence;
- people of untidy, dirty appearance, especially with dirty shoes;
- people who are nervous, too confident or servile in police presence (unless they are doctors, who are naturally confident);
- people whose appearance is abnormal in some way – e.g. their clothes are not as smart as their car;
- people in unusual family circumstances.

T P A Stereotyping

14 Describe what stereotype of offenders is obvious in doc. 8.

15 Consider how the police would stereotype you, your friends or relatives.

16 Police officers will tell you that these are no stereotypes but descriptions of people who were picked up for some offence or other.
Can you point out the dangers of taking such a view?

17 Point out other groups in society that have the power to label people. Give examples and explain the consequences of such labelling. Use docs. 6 and 7.

A A criminal crossword puzzle

18 Solve the puzzle and you will get a suspicious age group as the password (↓).

Clues:
(1) to keep someone in a prison
(2) the fear of being punished may ... someone from a crime
(3) children below 14 are not ... for their offences
(4) somebody who has committed an offence
(5) to stop someone from doing something
(6) a consequence of an offence
(7) people to whom a crime can be proved are ... of it
(8) a plain-clothes policeman
(9) somebody who breaks the law
(10) being in ... means being kept locked up in a cell
(11) as long as nothing can be proved to a criminal he or she is a ...

A case of shoplifting

For the thrill of it? (doc. 1)

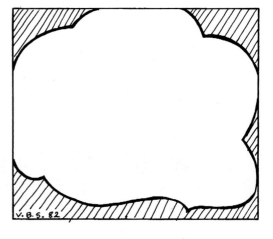

P A The price tag

1 Doc. 1 is a series of pictures. Turn this series of pictures into a story with a realistic ending.

2 What makes the girl an offender?

3 Look at doc. 3. Why are young girls tempted to steal from shops like the one below?

Shoplifting - A harmless offence?

If we take a look at German criminal statistics, the following picture emerges. Of all types of offences, theft – without or under aggravating circumstances – and criminal damage take top positions.
Theft without aggravating circumstances includes shoplifting and any theft that is committed without using force. Theft under aggravating circumstances includes burglary or the breaking of cigarette machines.

D A Investigating juvenile delinquency

4 Study doc. 2 and point out the frequency of various offences in the groups presented.

5 Draw a bar graph to show proportions of suspected offenders graphically.

Theft and criminal damage in Germany, 1992 (doc. 2)

The following example helps you to read and understand the table below. Of all offences which boys under fourteen were suspected, 62.9 % were thefts without aggravating circumstances.

offences	children		adolescents	
	male	female	male	female
theft without aggravating circumstances	62.9	80.6	46.6	65.5
theft under aggravating circumstances	12.8	4.0	19.5	4.3
criminal damage	15.6	5.8	14.2	4.3
other	8.7	9.6	19.7	25.9

Shopping in an expensive boutique (doc. 3)

Shoplifting in Germany, 1987–1992 (doc. 4)

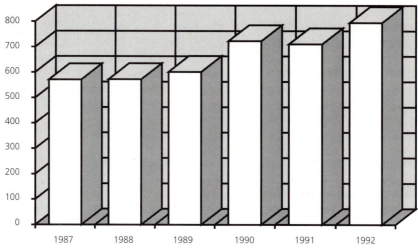

cases in 100,000 population

The damage done – Losses to German shopowners, 1992 (doc. 5)

value of stolen goods	below DM 25	DM 25 to DM 100	DM 100 to DM 1,000	DM 1,000 to DM 10,000	DM 10,000 to DM 100,000
percentage of total thefts	45.9	31.1	21.1	1.8	0.1

total losses to shopowners in 1992: DM 68.4 million

Sex and age of German shoplifters, 1992 (doc. 6)
(in actual figures)

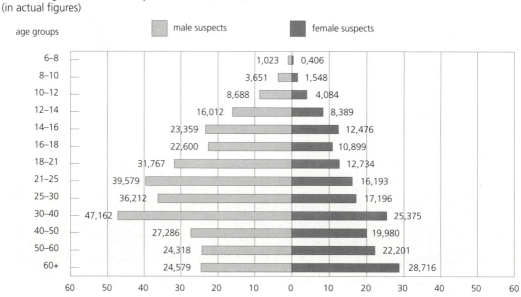

A Project: Shoplifting in Germany

6 Docs. 4 to 6 give information about various aspects of shoplifting in Germany. Analyse these documents and write a paragraph on each of these documents.
Think of a suitable order to connect your paragraphs. You will then get a full report on shoplifting in Germany.

Polly's case

Let us now turn to Pauline Waters. Pauline has broken the law and has been arrested for shoplifting. She has been prosecuted by the shop manager and is waiting for her trial at a juvenile court. She is a first offender and, like the great majority of these, will probably never have to appear before a court like the one below again.
This is Polly's criminal profile:

name:	Pauline Waters
age:	fourteen years, three months
school:	girls' grammar
offence:	stealing from an Oxford Street store (two cardigans and a pair of tights)
place of trial:	juvenile court.

C A People at a magistrate's court

7 Before you study Polly's trial, make sure you know about the roles of the various persons shown in doc. 7. If you are in doubt, consult your dictionary.
Then draw a chart in your exercise book and explain the various roles at a magistrate's court.

role	function at a trial
justices	...
prosecuting lawyer	...

1 chairman of justices
2 justices of the peace
3 clerk to the justices
4 prosecuting lawyer (seated)
5 defending lawyer (standing)
6 probation officers
7 defendant
8 police officer
9 usher
10 other witnesses
11 press
12 public

At a magistrate's court (doc. 7)

Polly's trial (doc. 8)

Usher: This is Polly, your worship, and her Mother.

[The chairman nods and Polly and Mrs Waters sit.]

Clerk: Age?

Polly: F-Fourteen and a half.

Clerk: Polly, you are charged with stealing two cardigans and a pair of tights from Allied Wholesalers Ltd. – do you understand what that means?

Polly: Yes.

Clerk: Do you admit stealing this clothing?

Polly: [very quiet]

Yes.

Magistrate: Who can give us the facts?

[W.P.C. Rodgers steps into the witness box]

Rodgers: W.P.C. Rodgers. At 11.35 a.m. on Saturday, 15 June 1968, I was called to Allied Wholesalers Ltd. store in Oxford Street by Mr Stevens, the manager, who said to me in Polly's presence, "This girl has just been caught stealing in the store. I'm fed up. It's the fifteenth loss this week. If it isn't foreign girls, it's our own." I cautioned her and said, "What have you to say?" She replied, "I'm sorry, do you have to tell my parents?"

[pause, W.P.C. Rodgers steps down from the box but stands ready to answer any questions.]

Clerk: Do you want to ask any questions, Polly?

[Polly shakes her head.]

Magistrate: Now Polly, what's all this about?

Clerk: Stand up.

Magistrate: [gently]

Come up here.

[Polly steps close to the bench.]

Polly: I meant to pay.

Magistrate: Then why didn't you?

[silence]

Did you have any money on you at the time?

Mrs Waters: I'd given her two pounds –

Magistrate: Is that true?

Polly: Yes.

Magistrate: If you'd only wanted one cardigan – you could have bought it – is that right?

[Polly nods.]

Then why did you need the extra one?

Polly: I didn't.

Magistrate: Polly, what I don't understand –

Polly: [defiant]

They said it was easy!

[pause]

Magistrate: What?

Polly: Going in ... and ... taking things.

Magistrate: Who are they?

Polly: The others. At school.

[defiant]

They've done it.

At the supermarket (doc. 9)

T A A youth court in session

8 In doc. 8, who is concerned with Polly during the trial? What do these people do?

9 The facts about Polly's case are known to the magistrate. Nevertheless, he keeps asking Polly questions. Explain why he does this and to what effect.

10 We finally hear what motive Polly had when she stole the clothes from the shop.
Write an additional scene with Polly and her classmates at school during which Polly develops the idea of stealing something at this shop.

11 What advice would you have given Polly if she had told you about her classmates?

12 Imagine you were one of the lay justices. What sentence would you pronounce at the end of her trial? Give reasons.

P A Sweet temptation - Effects of advertising

13 Doc. 9 shows a scene at a supermarket. As you can see, all posters advertising goods and special offers have been blanked out. Try to fill them with eye-catching slogans.

14 Imagine you are a manager of a supermarket. How would you design the posters in doc. 9? How would you arrange and put on display the items you want to sell?

15 Can you imagine that advertising may tempt people to take things from shelves without paying for them?
Why do you think children may be misled by advertising?

16 In what way does doc. 9 explain some of the statistical facts presented in docs. 4, 5 and 6?

In a detention centre (doc. 1)

Legal facts

The law in England and Wales

Children below ten years of age are believed not to be able to understand the difference between right and wrong. Therefore, they do not face criminal prosecution and no criminal proceedings will be brought against them. However, children between ten and fourteen may be prosecuted and brought before a youth court. If the prosecution can prove to the court that they are able to distinguish between right and wrong, they can be made responsible for what they have done.

Children between ten and fourteen years of age who are accused of less serious offences are tried in a youth court which is formed by three lay justices or magistrates. More serious cases (manslaughter, murder, etc.) are dealt with at crown courts by a jury if the prosecution has enough evidence.

Types of sentences

The most common types of sentences are:
- detention 'at Her Majesty's pleasure' (in very serious cases) or at young offenders' institutions (in serious cases);
- supervision orders with conditions;
- attendance centre orders;
- fines.

Detention 'at Her Majesty's pleasure': A child will be sent to one of the four special secure centres for an indefinite period of time. Boys between 14 and 16 may receive a custodial sentence and be sent to a young offenders' institution.

Supervision orders with conditions: In the vast majority of cases youth courts will suggest measures to help offenders and their parents. If youngsters are accused and found guilty of an offence, they will be put under the supervision of qualified social workers or probation officers for some time. During this time children may live at home.

In cases where the jury feels that parents are unable to cope with the young offenders, foster parents will have to be found. Supervision may mean that the child will have to obey certain orders or directions, such as taking part in special educational programmes.

- Attendance centre orders: If offenders are found guilty, youth courts may also rule that children will have to spend up to 24 hours of their leisure time at attendance centres. Physical education and instruction in practical subjects are provided there.

Instead of being sent to attendance centres, 16-year-old offenders may be ordered to do up to 120 hours of community service. This includes decorating the houses of elderly or disabled people or building playgrounds.

- Fines: The most common sentence will be a fine. The idea is to compensate for the damage that has been done. Of course, the offender should be able to pay the fine and not be forced to commit a second offence in order to pay the fine for the first.

G Legal facts - A flow chart

1 In order to understand the procedures better, copy the flow chart below into your exercise book and complete it.

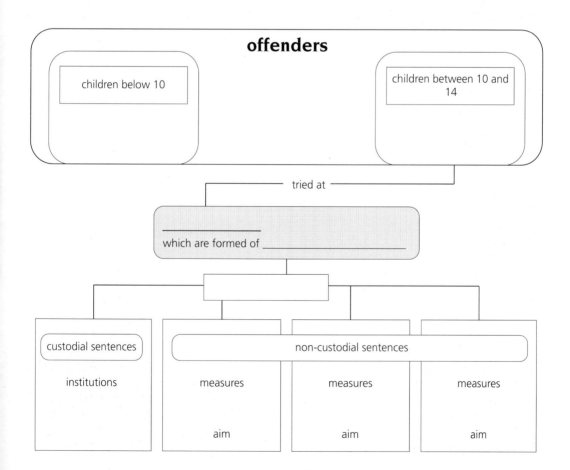

Causes of crime and violence

Young offenders in their own words
(doc. 1)

In this section we will be concerned with the background and some of the causes of crime. We will start with two statements made by offenders who have been sent to a London institution which specializes in dealing with persistent offenders, i.e. offenders who have repeatedly been caught by the police. This institution and the programmes it offers are their last chance. Should they stop attending courses or continue their criminal ways while they are there, they would be sent to prison immediately.

Johnny's statement:

I know stealing is wrong. I wouldn't want nobody taking my stuff. But it's money at the end of the day. I used to be an angel. When you're twelve, thirteen, you do a bit of shoplifting, say at Harrods, just for a laugh, or you smash bottles or play around with the police; well, I wouldn't do any of that. Then I bumped into a certain group of friends – influenced basically – that's when I started. They were into car stereos. Obviously, what your friends do, you do. (...)
Most people do things wrong but they don't consider themselves criminals. They drop litter, they speed, drive over the limit, it's wrong but they still do it. Stealing is wrong. I know that it's blatantly true. People say "well, they're too rich anyway." But if they've got things and they've worked hard and been lucky enough to make their life the way they want it, they're welcome to it. The only way someone like me is going to get rich is some deal that produces ten grand.

Joel's statement:

I reckon there's three categories: drug takers, drinkers, and straight people. But eighty per cent of the kids I know of around this area all take drugs. The other fifteen per cent just drink and say drugs are bad, though they have tried them, and the other five per cent don't do anything. That's just the way it goes. I've been taking drugs all my life, so I don't know any other way. I'm not really qualified to say if I'd like to be one of the five per cent or not. There is a part of me that thinks that I would, but I just couldn't live one of those lives, cos I'm not straight basically.
I suppose I think of myself as a criminal. In the eyes of everyone else I'm a criminal. I don't think about it. It's alright, know what I mean, it's just usual innit, normal? I steal for money, for clothes, for booze, for drugs – for life!

⬛ Offenders' backgrounds

1 Study doc. 1 carefully and answer the following questions.
a) What were Johnny's and Joel's motivations to become criminals?
b) How do the boys describe themselves?

2 Which of the boys seems to have a greater chance of stopping his criminal career? What makes you think so?

3 How can society help him to do so?

Growing up in an uncaring world

Biographies of the overwhelming majority of delinquents reveal that most of them did not enjoy a well-ordered and sheltered family life.
Recent FBI statistics show that 70 per cent of all juvenile offenders in the United States come from single-parent families. Since 1970 the number of single-parent homes has increased by 200 per cent.

The family history of a young offender
(doc. 2)

Bobby's parents had married in December 1971, both aged 18. Bobby was their fifth son. His father was an apprentice electrician, and there was little money and considerable worry. The marriage was volatile. He would sometimes hit his wife after he had been drinking. (...)

As the couple grew older, family life became more stable. They would all go on fishing trips and camping holidays together. In the summer holidays of 1988 they became friendly with another couple and Bobby's father eventually left to set up home with the other woman. The only time they saw him after that was at the grandmother's funeral.

Bobby's mother, Ann, had relied on her husband emotionally and financially; she was unprepared for his departure. She began drinking heavily, losing her grip on the family and getting into debt. The older boys were left in charge and sometimes hit the younger ones.

The older boys began truanting, hanging around with other lads in the area and getting involved in petty crime. Two were taken into care; the rest had to look after themselves at home.

TPA Lessons learned at home

4 Study docs. 2 and 3, then complete the diagram below, which shows how this boy experienced family life.
Doc. 2 will give you the information you need about the headwords in the boxes.

5 At the age of ten, Bobby and a friend of his brutally killed a boy of two after abducting and torturing him.
How may their minds have been prepared to commit a crime like this?

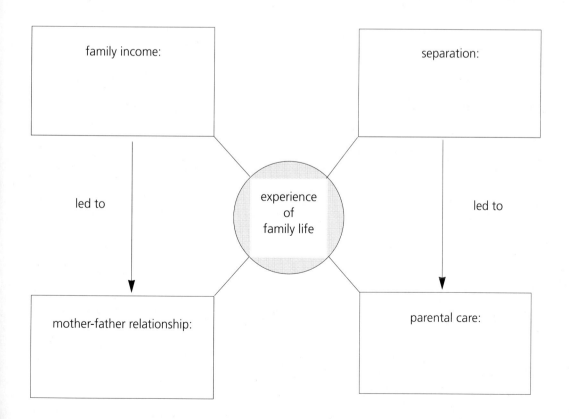

Blocks of flats in Chemnitz (doc. 3)

Families in Germany

In the former Federal Republic of Germany about 14 per cent of all marriages were annulled in 1960. This figure rose to 31 per cent in 1989, which means that one in three marriages is likely to fail and will end in a divorce court. In 1989 127,000 divorce cases deprived 90,000 children either of their mother or father, although in 52 per cent of all cases couples were without children. Usually courts will rule that children are to live with their mothers (85 per cent) who are supposed to be supported by their former husbands. However, there is also a growing number of single-parent families where children grow up with their fathers.

Doc. 4, which is based on figures compiled by the Statistisches Bundesamt, illustrates the trend in the number of single-parent families in Germany.

Changes in family life

Apart from a rise in the number of single-parent families, family life has undergone some important changes. The traditional family, with a male breadwinner and the housewife looking after the children, does no longer exist. More and more women have sought employment.

In Germany in 1990, 90.4 per cent of all women without children between the ages of 25 and 30 and 65.3 per cent of those with children (between 6 and 15 years of age) had a job. In the United States the number of married mothers who leave home for work every morning rose by 65 per cent between 1970 and 1990. The number of children who have to prepare their own meals every day more than doubled between 1987 and 1993.

Single-parent families in Germany, 1970–1992 (doc. 4)

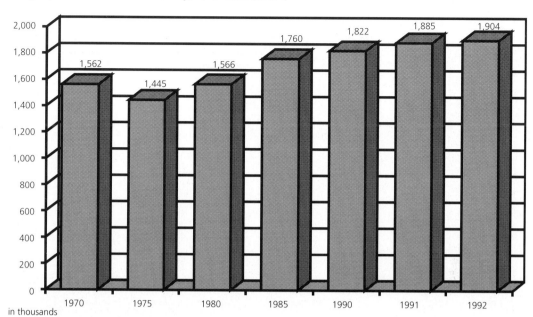

in thousands

- 1970: 1,562
- 1975: 1,445
- 1980: 1,566
- 1985: 1,760
- 1990: 1,822
- 1991: 1,885
- 1992: 1,904

🆖 When parents separate

6 Use the figures in doc. 4 to calculate the rate by which the number of single-parent families has grown from 1970 to 1992.
Draw a line graph onto doc. 4, which shows the changes against the previous years in percentage. Add a second y-axis for the percentages.

7 Describe developments in the number of single-parent families over the period from 1970 to 1992. Use doc. 4 and the two texts on the opposite page.

8 What problems do children have to face when parents separate?

Home-alone children in Britain (doc. 5)

According to a study presented at the Conference of British Geographers in January 1994, "home alone" children "are now part of the British way of life." The following passages are parts of an interview with the author of this study, Miss Fiona Smith of Reading University.

"About one in five parents leave children under 11 on their own for hours after school, or for the entire day during holidays. The mothers often feel guilty and worried, cannot work properly and may telephone their children several times each hour. The children are ordered to stay indoors.(...)
The parents say they have no choice; they need to work to pay the mortgage and feed their families. Most parents, including those who left their children at home, felt they should not be alone until the age of 13 or 14. Many working mothers with unaccompanied children at home would take jobs only within 10 minutes of their houses to be able to attend quickly in an emergency. (...)
Some of the children said they quite liked being able to do their own thing, but many were bored because they were not allowed to go outside."

Working women in Germany, 1962 and 1990 (doc. 6)

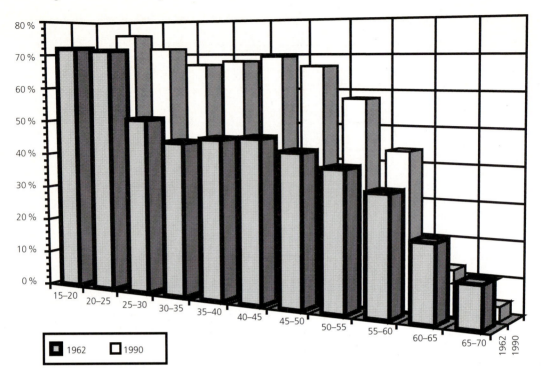

🆃🅖 How children's homes have changed

9 Explain why more and more children are no longer looked after by either of their parents for most time of the day. Doc. 5 will help you.

10 Have a close look at doc. 6.
a) What conclusions can you draw from the diagram about family life in the 1960s and in the 1990s?
b) Explain why the proportion of women in employment is different in particular age groups.

11 In 1962, how was family life organized after the birth of children? What changes have taken place?

12 How do parents and children feel about the present situation? How do you think unaccompanied children spend their time at home?

13 Do you think the suggestions in doc. 7 might solve the problem of home-alone children?

Wages for mothers? (doc. 7)

On February 23, 1993, the Evening Standard published the following letter to the editor. The letter was written by Dame Barbara Cartland, a successful writer of romance novels, who comments on the question of 'How to save our children from crime.'

We must be aware that the fault comes from the fact that the vast majority of young criminals come from broken homes. I have been, for the last three years, fighting for wages for wives in this country. This means that the mother is paid to stay at home with her children for the first five years until they go to school.
The child then, when it is very young, would receive the love which all children need, and also the feeling of security. Children who are deprived of this easily become juvenile criminals because they have never been loved or experienced any form of home life.

Childhood in the video age (doc. 8)

Through television and video, images of unspeakable brutality have now entered even the most secure and protected homes. Miss Wright, who has taught for 11 years in Silver Spring, Maryland, notices a "major difference" when it comes to the stories her students now choose to tell. Today, "eyes are being pulled out, arms chopped off, heads cut off ... usually the story ends with a death."

Does this mean that the children who recount these tales will grow up to become violent criminals? Of course not. But no sane society can remain unconcerned when the traditional fantasies of childhood – of talking animals, fairy godmothers and magical journeys – are replaced by images of mutilation and mayhem, which are then proudly shared with teachers and schoolmates.

* In February 1993 two 10-year-old boys were charged with and found guilty of the abduction and murder of two-year old toddler James Bulger in Liverpool. They were sentenced to be detained at "Her Majesty's pleasure" at a secure centre for an indefinite period of time. Doc. 2 on page 21 also refers to the Bulger case.

Such bloody images are once again the focus of intense debate after the James Bulger murder case*. "It isn't for me to pass judgement on their upbringing," said Mr Justice Morland of the killers. "But I suspect that exposure to violent video films may, in part, be an explanation." Of course, it is impossible to prove him definitely right or wrong in this case. (...)

The fact that violent imagery fails to influence everyone does not mean that it fails to influence anyone. Movie mayhem does not have to damage all members of the audience in order to damage our overall quality of life. Even if it is only a few thousand – or a few hundred – vulnerable individuals who are encouraged to commit murderous cruelty by the bloody messages of the popular culture, the impact on society can be enormous.

D Recent figures

14 According to the American Psychological Association, the average child watches 8,000 televised murders and 100,000 acts of violence before finishing elementary school. How many on average is that per week/day?

Televisions for sale (doc. 9)

Children and TV in Britain (doc. 10)

In Britain a study of 20,000 children aged 11 to 14 was published at Exeter University in 1993. The following passages summarize some of its findings.

For many, television is a form of escape: a quarter told the researchers that they watched it as a way of easing anxieties. Most spend up to two hours a night after school watching programmes, often away from parents on sets in their bedroom. (...)
At least a fifth of the girls said that they had very little to do in their spare time. Almost as many boys were bored, preferring television to reading a book, doing homework or playing outside.
Up to one in six admitted to having watched more than three hours television the previous night. For one in three, it was more than two hours. Girls watch only slightly less and are more likely than boys to do homework or read books.
The importance of television was evident among pupils last week at Fearnhill School, a co-educational comprehensive in Letchworth, Hertfordshire, which has examination results above the national average and hardly any truancy.
Amanda Hardwick, 14, had watched more than two hours television the previous night after doing homework. Her favourites were serials and soaps, such as 'Neighbours' and 'Home and Away.' "I feel pressured into having to watch certain programmes. All my friends watch them. If I don't, I feel left out," she said.

T D P Lessons learned from the screen

15 According to doc. 8, how do teachers in the USA notice changes in children's imagination? What observations do they make?

16 Does the author think that watching brutality on TV creates criminal minds? Explain.

17 Look at task 14 again. Can you imagine what effect regular TV watching can have on young minds?

18 What makes TV so attractive to young people? Use docs. 9 and 10.

A Project: TV at home

19 Examine the TV viewing habits in your class.
a) How many hours per day/week do students watch television?
b) What are the favourite programmes? Why do students like to watch them?
c) Which programmes contain violence?

Bottled-up fury (doc. 11)

The following excerpt from Stan Barstow's short story 'The Desperadoes' adds another aspect to the range of causes of delinquency.

What started it that night was the row Vince had with his father. He couldn't remember just what began the row itself, but something like it seemed to blow up every time the Old Man saw him, and started using expressions like 'idle layabout,' 'lazy good-for-nothing' and 'no-good little teddy boy.' The Old Man never talked to you – he talked at you; he didn't carry on a conversation – he told you things.
When Vince stormed out of the house, he hardly knew where he was going; he was so full of bottled-up fury. Violence writhed within him like a trapped and vicious snake.
He felt like kicking in the teeth of the first person who might glance twice at him, and he thought that perhaps the easiest way of relieving his feelings would be to find the boys and go smash up a few chairs at the Youth Club. Except that that might bring a copper to the door and he got on the wrong side of the Old Man easily enough without having the police help along.

T/A The "vicious snake" of rage

20 Describe how Vince's anger grows in doc. 11. What outlet does he seek for his "bottled-up fury?"

21 Explain his father's attitude towards Vince.

22 Have you ever been in a situation similar to the one above? What was its background? What was the outcome?

P/A Understanding violent behaviour

23 Have a close look at doc. 12, then write a story about these pictures.

24 What – in sociological terms – is happening? The text "Why people become aggressive" will help you.

25 Explain Vince's behaviour in doc. 11. Use evidence from any document in this chapter.

Why people become aggressive

Sociologists and psychologists have given a lot of thought to what causes people to be violent and aggressive. Here are some explanations they found.

Whenever people realize that a particular way of solving a problem appears to be successful, they will learn to use this method very quickly. If they grow up in an environment of aggressiveness and violence which teaches them that only the most ruthless people will be successful, they will soon follow their example and become violent themselves.

Apart from these explanations of why people become aggressive and violent at times, there is one theory which claims that many people react aggressively if they have experienced some kind of frustration before. Everybody's hopes and expectations are frustrated from time to time. Normally, people are able to keep feelings of anger or disappointment under control.

However, there are limits, and sometimes it only takes an unimportant remark or gesture from somebody else to let these feelings out in a violent act – mostly directed at victims who can hardly be made responsible for the anger or frustration. People appear to be looking for scapegoats for their frustrations, especially if they do not dare to express their true feelings. Examples are when people are treated unfairly by superiors or when they do not get what they want.

Taking it out (doc. 12)

Glossary

English - German

to **abduct**	entführen
acceptable	akzeptabel, angemessen
adolescent	Jugendliche(r)
adult, grown-up	Erwachsener
aggravating circumstances	erschwerende Bedingungen
aggressiveness	Aggressivität
to **annul (a marriage)**	annullieren, tilgen, aufheben
anxiety	Angst, Besorgnis
to **arrest, detain, incarcerate s.b.**	jdn. einsperren, unter Arrest stellen
assault	Überfall
to **be accused (of)**	beschuldigt werden
to **be arrested**	festgenommen werden
to **be concerned with**	mit etwas befaßt sein
to **be guilty (of an offence)**	schuldig sein
to **be prosecuted**	angezeigt, verfolgt werden
to **be remanded (in custody)**	in Untersuchungshaft gehalten werden
to **be suspected (of)**	verdächtigt werden
block of flats	Wohnblock
(bottled-up) fury	(aufgestaute) Wut
to **bring criminal proceedings against s.b.**	gegen jdn. ein Strafverfahren einleiten
brutality	Brutalität
burglary	Einbruch
car wreck	Autowrack
case	Fall
to **charge s.b. (with), bring charges against s.b.**	jdn. anklagen, beschuldigen
code of conduct	Verhaltenskodex
community service	Gemeindedienst
to **compensate (for)**	entschädigen, wiedergutmachen
conception (of)	Vorstellung (von)
to **confirm**	bestätigen
copper	umgangssprachl.: Polizist, Bulle
courtroom	Gerichtssaal
crime	Straftat, Verbrechen
criminal	Kriminelle(r)
criminal damage	Sachbeschädigung
criminal offence	kriminelle Straftat
criminal statistics	Kriminalstatistik
defendant	Angeklagte(r)
defending lawyer	Verteidiger
delinquent	Straffällige(r)
to **deprive (s.b. of)**	jdn. einer Sache berauben
detention	Freiheitsstrafe
deterrent	Abschreckung(smittel)
deviance	abweichendes Verhalten
deviant	abweichend
to **disapprove (of)**	ablehnen
divorce	Scheidung
eviction	Räumung
evidence	Beweis(mittel), Indizien
for sale	zu verkaufen
foster parents	Pflegeeltern
frequency	Häufigkeit
frustration	Frustration, Enttäuschung
home-alone children	Schlüsselkinder
hooligan	Rowdy
illegal	ungesetzlich, illegal
indecent	ungehörig, unanständig
instruction material	Unterrichtsmaterial

joyride	Spritztour (mit einem gestohlenen Auto)	rage	Zorn
justice, judge, magistrate	Richter	retribution	Vergeltung
		robbery	Raub
juvenile delinquency youth crime	Jugendkriminalität	row, quarrel	Streit, Auseinandersetzung
juvenile court, youth court	Jugendgericht	ruthless	rücksichtslos
		scapegoat	Prügelknabe
		sentence	Urteil
to keep s.b. in custody	jdn. gefangen halten	shoplifting	Ladendiebstahl
		single-parent family	alleinerziehende Familie
to label s.b.	jdn. in eine Schublade stecken, etikettieren	social service department	hier: Jugendamt
law	Gesetz	stereotype	Stereotype
		supervision order	gerichtlich verfügte Beaufsichtigung eines Straftäters
magistrate's court	Amtsgericht		
to make/hold s.b. responsible (for)	jdn. für etwas verantwortlich machen	suspect	Verdächtige(r)
mayhem	schwere Körperverletzung	to suspect s.b. (of)	jdn. verdächtigen
		suspicious	verdächtig
mutilation	Verstümmelung		
		to take it out	sich abreagieren
norm	Norm, Richtschnur	to take offence (at)	Anstoß nehmen (an)
		theft	Diebstahl
		to torture	quälen
offence	Straftat, Vergehen	trait (of character), characteristic	Charakterzug
offender	Straftäter(in)		
offensive	anstößig, abstoßend	trial	Gerichtsverhandlung
orders and directions	Auflagen und Weisungen	to try an offence (in court)	eine Strafsache verhandeln
outrageous	ungeheuerlich		
		up against the wall	mit dem Rücken zur Wand
to pass judgement (on)	beurteilen		
persistent offender	Wiederholungstäter	vicious	bösartig
to prevent (s.b. from)	jdn. abhalten von	victim	Opfer
price tag	Preisschild	to violate (the rules)	(die Regeln) verletzen
to pronounce (a sentence)	verkünden		
proof	Beweis	wages	Lohn
proportion	Anteil (von)	Who dunnit?	Wer war der Täter?
prosecuting lawyer	Ankläger(in)	witness	Zeuge
prosecution	Anklage		
to prove	beweisen		
to punish	bestrafen		
to put s.b. under supervision	jdn. unter Aufsicht stellen		

German - English

jdn. **abhalten von**	to prevent (s.b. from)
ablehnen	to disapprove (of)
sich **abreagieren**	to take it out
Abschreckung(smittel)	deterrent
abweichend	deviant
abweichendes Verhalten	deviance
Aggressivität	aggressiveness
akzeptabel, angemessen	acceptable
alleinerziehende Familie	single-parent family
Amtsgericht	magistrate's court
Anstoß nehmen (an)	to take offence (at)
anstößig, abstoßend	offensive
Angeklagte(r)	defendant
angezeigt, verfolgt werden	to be prosecuted
Angst, Besorgnis	anxiety
Anklage	prosecution
jdn. **anklagen, beschuldigen**	to charge s.b. (with), bring charges against s.b.
Ankläger(in)	prosecuting lawyer
annullieren, tilgen, aufheben	to annul (a marriage)
Anteil (von)	proportion
(aufgestaute) Wut	(bottled-up) fury
Auflagen und Weisungen	orders and directions
Autowrack	car wreck
beschuldigt werden	to be accused (of)
bestätigen	to confirm
bestrafen	to punish
beurteilen	to pass judgement (on)
Beweis	proof
beweisen	to prove
Beweis(mittel), Indizien	evidence
bösartig	vicious
Brutalität	brutality
Charakterzug	trait (of character), characteristic
Diebstahl	theft
Einbruch	burglary
jdn. **einer Sache berauben**	to deprive (s.b. of)
jdn. **einsperren, unter Arrest stellen**	to arrest, detain, incarcerate s.b.
entführen	to abduct
entschädigen, wiedergutmachen	to compensate (for)
erschwerende Bedingungen	aggravating circumstances
Erwachsener	adult, grown-up
Fall	case
festgenommen werden	to be arrested
Freiheitsstrafe	detention
Frustration, Enttäuschung	frustration
jdn. **gefangen halten**	to keep s.b. in custody
Gemeindedienst	community service
gerichtlich verfügte Beaufsichtigung eines Straftäters	supervision order
Gerichtssaal	courtroom
Gerichtsverhandlung	trial
Gesetz	law
Häufigkeit	frequency
jdn. **in eine Schublade stecken, etikettieren**	to label s.b.
Jugendamt	social service department
Jugendgericht	juvenile/youth court
Jugendkriminalität	juvenile delinquency, youth crime
Jugendliche(r)	adolescent
Kriminalstatistik	criminal statistics

Kriminelle(r)	criminal
kriminelle Straftat	criminal offence
Ladendiebstahl	shoplifting
Lohn	wages
mit etwas befaßt sein	to be concerned with
mit dem Rücken zur Wand	up against the wall
Norm, Richtschnur	norm
Opfer	victim
Pflegeeltern	foster parents
Polizist, Bulle	umgangssprachl.: copper
Preisschild	price tag
Prügelknabe	scapegoat
quälen	to torture
Raub	robbery
Räumung	eviction
(die Regeln) verletzen	to violate (the rules)
Richter	justice, judge, magistrate
Rowdy	hooligan
rücksichtslos	ruthless
Sachbeschädigung	criminal damage
Scheidung	divorce
Schlüsselkinder	home-alone children
schuldig sein	to be guilty (of an offence)
schwere Körperverletzung	mayhem
Spritztour (mit einem gestohlenen Auto)	joyride
Stereotype	stereotype
Straffällige(r)	delinquent
eine **Strafsache verhandeln**	to try an offence (in court)
Straftat, Verbrechen	crime
Straftat, Vergehen	offence
Straftäter(in)	offender
gegen jdn. ein **Strafverfahren einleiten**	to bring criminal proceedings against s.b.
Streit, Auseinandersetzung	row, quarrel
Überfall	assault
ungeheuerlich	outrageous
ungehörig, unanständig	indecent
ungesetzlich, illegal	illegal
jdn. **unter Aufsicht stellen**	to put s.b. under supervision
Unterrichtsmaterial	instruction material
in **Untersuchungshaft gehalten werden**	to be remanded (in custody)
Urteil	sentence
jdn. **verantwortlich machen**	to make/hold s.b. responsible (for)
verdächtig	suspicious
jdn. **verdächtigen**	to suspect s.b. (of)
Verdächtige(r)	suspect
verdächtigt werden	to be suspected (of)
Vergeltung	retribution
Verhaltenskodex	code of conduct
verkünden	to pronounce (a sentence)
Verstümmelung	mutilation
Verteidiger	defending lawyer
vom Gericht verfügte Beaufsichtigung eines Straftäters	supervision order
Vorstellung (von)	conception (of)
Wer war der Täter?	umgangssprachl.: Who dunnit?
Wiederholungstäter	persistent offender
Wohnblock	block of flats
Zeuge	witness
Zorn	rage
zu verkaufen	for sale

Bild- und Textquellen

2.1 Wintrup Musikverlag, Detmold – 3.2/Umschlag GAMMA, Paris (Sion) – 4.3 "Sociology: A Modular Approach," by Denis Gleeson, Oxford, OUP, 1990, p. 234, reprinted by permission of Oxford University Press – 6.1 John Furbisher, The Sunday Times, 14.2.1993, (c) Times Newspapers Ltd., 1993 – 7.2 dpa, Frankfurt (Fuehler) – 10.7 Mansell Collection, London – 11.8 (c) McGraw Hill Europe, Maidenhead – 12.1 Ministerium für Arbeit, Gesundheit und Soziales des Landes Nordrhein-Westfalen – 13.3 Das Fotoarchiv, Essen (Christoph) – 15.7 "Law and Order in the 1990's," by Les Fargie, published by W & R Chambers Ltd – 16.8/profile on page 15 "Connexions: The Lawbreakers," by Ray Jenkins, Penguin Books, 1969, pp. 20, 27-29, (c) 1969 by Ray Jenkins, reproduced by permission of Penguin Books Ltd – 17.9 Ministerium für Arbeit, Gesundheit und Soziales des Landes Nordrhein-Westfalen – 18.1 GAMMA, Paris – 20.1 material used with permission of Harper Collins Publishers, material taken from "Living Dangerously: Young Offenders in their own Words," by (c) Roger Graef – 21.2 David James Smith, "The Sleep of Reason," Century – 22.3 Visum, Hamburg (Ludwig) – 23.5 by permission of The Independent (6.1.1994) – 24.7 (c) Barbara Cartland, 1993 – 25.8 by Michael Medved – 25.9 Topham/Picture Point, Edenbridge – 26.10 Charles Hymes, The Sunday Times, 28.2.1993, (c) Times Newspapers Ltd., 1993 – 26.11 "The Desperadoes," by Stan Barstow, London, Corgi 1974, p. 154, (c) Stan Barstow, 1974, reproduced by permission of Penguin Books Ltd. – 27.12 "Connexions: Violence, Its Nature, Causes and Remedies," edited by Colin War, Penguin Books, 1970, p. 6, (c) Malcolm Bird, 1970, reproduced by permission of Penguin Books Ltd.

Every effort has been made to trace owners of copyright material. However, in a few cases this has not proved possible and enquiries have remained unanswered. The publishers would be glad to hear from any such owners of material reproduced in this booklet.